D1195600

THIS BOOK BELONGS TO

,,,

Thanks you for being our Valued Customer.We
would be grateful If you shared this happy
experience on amazon. This helps us to continue
providing great products,and helps potential
buyers to make confident decisions

By CAREEM BUFFET

"What is lovely never dies,
but passes into another
loveliness, Star-dust or sea-
foam, Flower or winged air."
– Thomas Bailey Aldrich

"What we have once enjoyed we can never lose. All that we love deeply becomes a part of us."

Helen Keller

•"Like a bird singing in the rain, let grateful memories survive in time of sorrow."
Robert Louis Stevenson

•"What we have once enjoyed we can never lose. All that we love deeply becomes a part of us." Helen Keller

•"Only a moment you stayed, but what an imprint your footprints have left on our hearts."
Dorothy Ferguson

•"He spoke well who said that graves are the footprints of angels."
Henry Wadsworth Longfellow

•"A great soul serves everyone all the time. A great soul never dies. It brings us together again and again."
Maya Angelou

•"If I had a flower for every time I thought of you,
I could walk in my garden forever."
Alfred Lord Tennyson

•"Unable are the loved to die, for love is immortality."
Emily Dickinson

•"There are no goodbyes for us. Wherever you are, you will always be in my heart."
Mahatma Gandhi

_____

•"Like a bird singing in the rain, let grateful
memories survive in time of sorrow."
Robert Louis Stevenson

•"What we have once enjoyed we can never lose.
All that we love deeply becomes a part of us."
Helen Keller

•"Only a moment you stayed, but what an imprint your footprints have left on our hearts."
Dorothy Ferguson

•"He spoke well who said that graves are the footprints of angels."
Henry Wadsworth Longfellow

•"A great soul serves everyone all the time. A great soul never dies. It brings us together again and again."
Maya Angelou

•"If I had a flower for every time I thought of you, I could walk in my garden forever."
Alfred Lord Tennyson

•"Unable are the loved to die, for love is immortality."
Emily Dickinson

•"There are no goodbyes for us. Wherever you are, you will always be in my heart."
Mahatma Gandhi

•"Like a bird singing in the rain, let grateful memories survive in time of sorrow."
Robert Louis Stevenson

•"What we have once enjoyed we can never lose.
All that we love deeply becomes a part of us."
Helen Keller

•"Only a moment you stayed, but what an imprint your footprints have left on our hearts."
Dorothy Ferguson

•"He spoke well who said that graves are the footprints of angels."
Henry Wadsworth Longfellow

•"A great soul serves everyone all the time. A great soul never dies. It brings us together again and again."
Maya Angelou

•"If I had a flower for every time I thought of you,
I could walk in my garden forever."
Alfred Lord Tennyson

•"Unable are the loved to die, for love is immortality."
Emily Dickinson

•"There are no goodbyes for us. Wherever you are, you will always be in my heart."
Mahatma Gandhi

•"Like a bird singing in the rain, let grateful memories survive in time of sorrow."
Robert Louis Stevenson

•"What we have once enjoyed we can never lose.
All that we love deeply becomes a part of us."
Helen Keller

•"Only a moment you stayed, but what an imprint your footprints have left on our hearts."
Dorothy Ferguson

•"He spoke well who said that graves are the footprints of angels."
Henry Wadsworth Longfellow

•"A great soul serves everyone all the time. A great soul never dies. It brings us together again and again."
Maya Angelou

•"If I had a flower for every time I thought of you,
I could walk in my garden forever."
Alfred Lord Tennyson

•"Unable are the loved to die, for love is immortality."
Emily Dickinson

•"There are no goodbyes for us. Wherever you are, you will always be in my heart."
Mahatma Gandhi

•"Like a bird singing in the rain, let grateful memories survive in time of sorrow."
Robert Louis Stevenson

•"What we have once enjoyed we can never lose.
All that we love deeply becomes a part of us."
Helen Keller

•"Only a moment you stayed, but what an imprint your footprints have left on our hearts."
Dorothy Ferguson

•"He spoke well who said that graves are the footprints of angels."
Henry Wadsworth Longfellow

•"A great soul serves everyone all the time. A great soul never dies. It brings us together again and again."
Maya Angelou

•"If I had a flower for every time I thought of you,
I could walk in my garden forever."
Alfred Lord Tennyson

•"Unable are the loved to die, for love is immortality."
Emily Dickinson

•"There are no goodbyes for us. Wherever you are, you will always be in my heart."
Mahatma Gandhi

•"Like a bird singing in the rain, let grateful memories survive in time of sorrow."
Robert Louis Stevenson

•"What we have once enjoyed we can never lose.
All that we love deeply becomes a part of us."
Helen Keller

•"Only a moment you stayed, but what an imprint your footprints have left on our hearts."
Dorothy Ferguson

•"He spoke well who said that graves are the footprints of angels."
Henry Wadsworth Longfellow

•"A great soul serves everyone all the time. A great soul never dies. It brings us together again and again."
Maya Angelou

•"If I had a flower for every time I thought of you,
I could walk in my garden forever."
Alfred Lord Tennyson

•"Unable are the loved to die, for love is immortality."
Emily Dickinson

•"There are no goodbyes for us. Wherever you are, you will always be in my heart."
Mahatma Gandhi

•"Like a bird singing in the rain, let grateful memories survive in time of sorrow."
Robert Louis Stevenson

•"What we have once enjoyed we can never lose. All that we love deeply becomes a part of us." Helen Keller

•"Only a moment you stayed, but what an imprint your footprints have left on our hearts."
Dorothy Ferguson

•"He spoke well who said that graves are the footprints of angels."
Henry Wadsworth Longfellow

•"A great soul serves everyone all the time. A great soul never dies. It brings us together again and again."
Maya Angelou

•"If I had a flower for every time I thought of you,
I could walk in my garden forever."
Alfred Lord Tennyson

•"Unable are the loved to die, for love is immortality."
Emily Dickinson

•"There are no goodbyes for us. Wherever you are, you will always be in my heart."
Mahatma Gandhi

•"Like a bird singing in the rain, let grateful memories survive in time of sorrow."
Robert Louis Stevenson

•"What we have once enjoyed we can never lose. All that we love deeply becomes a part of us." Helen Keller

•"Only a moment you stayed, but what an imprint your footprints have left on our hearts."
Dorothy Ferguson

•"He spoke well who said that graves are the footprints of angels."
Henry Wadsworth Longfellow

•"A great soul serves everyone all the time. A great soul never dies. It brings us together again and again."
Maya Angelou

•"If I had a flower for every time I thought of you,
I could walk in my garden forever."
Alfred Lord Tennyson

•"Unable are the loved to die, for love is immortality."
Emily Dickinson

•"There are no goodbyes for us. Wherever you are, you will always be in my heart."
Mahatma Gandhi

•"Like a bird singing in the rain, let grateful memories survive in time of sorrow."
Robert Louis Stevenson

•"What we have once enjoyed we can never lose.
All that we love deeply becomes a part of us."
Helen Keller

•"Only a moment you stayed, but what an imprint your footprints have left on our hearts."
Dorothy Ferguson

•"He spoke well who said that graves are the footprints of angels."
Henry Wadsworth Longfellow

•"A great soul serves everyone all the time. A great soul never dies. It brings us together again and again."
Maya Angelou

•"If I had a flower for every time I thought of you,
I could walk in my garden forever."
Alfred Lord Tennyson

•"Unable are the loved to die, for love is immortality."
Emily Dickinson

•"There are no goodbyes for us. Wherever you are, you will always be in my heart."
Mahatma Gandhi

•"Like a bird singing in the rain, let grateful memories survive in time of sorrow."
Robert Louis Stevenson

•"What we have once enjoyed we can never lose. All that we love deeply becomes a part of us." Helen Keller

•"Only a moment you stayed, but what an imprint your footprints have left on our hearts."
Dorothy Ferguson

•"He spoke well who said that graves are the footprints of angels."
Henry Wadsworth Longfellow

•"A great soul serves everyone all the time. A great soul never dies. It brings us together again and again."
Maya Angelou

•"If I had a flower for every time I thought of you,
I could walk in my garden forever."
Alfred Lord Tennyson

•"Unable are the loved to die, for love is immortality."
Emily Dickinson

•"There are no goodbyes for us. Wherever you are, you will always be in my heart."
Mahatma Gandhi

•"Like a bird singing in the rain, let grateful memories survive in time of sorrow."
Robert Louis Stevenson

•"What we have once enjoyed we can never lose.
All that we love deeply becomes a part of us."
Helen Keller

•"Only a moment you stayed, but what an imprint your footprints have left on our hearts."
Dorothy Ferguson

•"He spoke well who said that graves are the footprints of angels."
Henry Wadsworth Longfellow

•"A great soul serves everyone all the time. A great soul never dies. It brings us together again and again."
Maya Angelou

•"If I had a flower for every time I thought of you,
I could walk in my garden forever."
Alfred Lord Tennyson

•"Unable are the loved to die, for love is immortality."
Emily Dickinson

•"There are no goodbyes for us. Wherever you are, you will always be in my heart."
Mahatma Gandhi

•"Like a bird singing in the rain, let grateful memories survive in time of sorrow."
Robert Louis Stevenson

•"What we have once enjoyed we can never lose. All that we love deeply becomes a part of us." Helen Keller

•"Only a moment you stayed, but what an imprint your footprints have left on our hearts."
Dorothy Ferguson

•"He spoke well who said that graves are the footprints of angels."
Henry Wadsworth Longfellow

•"A great soul serves everyone all the time. A great soul never dies. It brings us together again and again."
Maya Angelou

•"If I had a flower for every time I thought of you,
I could walk in my garden forever."
Alfred Lord Tennyson

•"Unable are the loved to die, for love is immortality."
Emily Dickinson

•"There are no goodbyes for us. Wherever you are, you will always be in my heart."
Mahatma Gandhi

•"Like a bird singing in the rain, let grateful memories survive in time of sorrow."
Robert Louis Stevenson

•"What we have once enjoyed we can never lose.
All that we love deeply becomes a part of us."
Helen Keller

•"Only a moment you stayed, but what an imprint your footprints have left on our hearts."
Dorothy Ferguson

•"He spoke well who said that graves are the footprints of angels."
Henry Wadsworth Longfellow

•"A great soul serves everyone all the time. A great soul never dies. It brings us together again and again."
Maya Angelou

•"If I had a flower for every time I thought of you,
I could walk in my garden forever."
Alfred Lord Tennyson

•"Unable are the loved to die, for love is immortality."
Emily Dickinson

•"There are no goodbyes for us. Wherever you are, you will always be in my heart."
Mahatma Gandhi

•"Like a bird singing in the rain, let grateful memories survive in time of sorrow."
Robert Louis Stevenson

•"A great soul serves everyone all the time. A great soul never dies. It brings us together again and again."
Maya Angelou

•"If I had a flower for every time I thought of you,
I could walk in my garden forever."
Alfred Lord Tennyson